Contents

1 Sharon Stone

Sharon Stone is a Hollywood star.
It seems like
she has been a star for a long time.
It took her 12 years
and 16 films
to get to the top.

For some people
she is just another sexy actress.
Yet she has a Golden Globe Award
and an Oscar nomination
to her credit.

Sharon Stone with her Golden Globe Award.

It has been hard work
for Sharon to get to the top!
She is often said to be difficult.
She says what she thinks.
She is often mocked by people
and not very often praised by them.

She gets parts in films
because she is very glamorous
but she is a better actress
than many give her credit for.

2 Childhood

Sharon was born on 10 March 1958
in a small town in Pennsylvania.
She was the second of four children.
She grew up in a close family
but she didn't fit in.

As a little girl
Sharon was very serious.
At school play times she read books.
Adults could not
answer all Sharon's questions.
Her IQ was very high.
This means she was very clever.
She was the cleverest child in her class.

Sharon Stone as a teenager.

In the small working class town
where Sharon grew up,
she learned how to shoot,
fish and fix cars,
just like her two brothers.
She was a tomboy.

When Sharon was 13 years old
she rode her pony
into a washing line.
The line cut her neck.
The scar is still there today.

3 Dreams of Hollywood

Films were the love of Sharon's life
when she was a teenager.
Sharon was tall and thin.
She had dull hair and thick glasses
but she said she was going to be a star.

Sharon knew she had to
change her looks.
She turned to magazines for help.
She dyed her hair different colours
until she settled for blonde.
Then she changed
her glasses for contact lenses and exercised.
All she wanted to do
was to go to Hollywood and be a star.

In 1975 she went to college early,
but she was still
in front of the other students.
Also that year she won her first beauty contest.

Her prize took her to the city
and gave her the chance
to be a model.
At the age of 18 she left home
and went to New York
to join the famous
Ford model agency.

Sharon Stone – before the big time.

4 A Modelling Career

Modelling took Sharon
all round the world.
She was one of Ford's ten highest paid models
but she never let it get out of hand.
Sharon saved her money
while others were going to parties.
She knew about the dangers of a fast life.
Her brother Michael went to jail
for drug smuggling.

After a while Sharon asked herself
'Why am I doing this?'.
So she went back to New York
and took acting lessons.
She still wanted to be in films.

5 Early Days in Films

Sharon's start in acting
came in 1980.
She was in an advert for Diet Coke
and she had a small part in a film.
All she had to do was
kiss a window.

After this small start,
Sharon moved to Hollywood.
She only had the money for a small flat.

She needed to earn more
to pay for a better flat.
She told people
'I want to work with Robert De Niro'.
She needed money
so she worked on a long line of bad films.

Sharon in *Tripple Trouble*, May 1984.

Sharon admits that back then
she needed a good manager.
She was seen as a dumb blonde.
In Hollywood, some people think that
blonde women are not intelligent.
Sharon is both.

By 1989 she had a string of bad films
and a failed marriage behind her.
She got herself a new agent
and tried to get parts in big films,
like *Batman*
but she was turned down.
Then she was sent the script
of an action film.

At first she said, 'No'.
Then she found out the film had a top star
and a big budget.
So she said, 'Yes'.

The film was *Total Recall*
and the star was Arnold Schwarzenegger.

Sharon had to go into training
in the gym for the film.
She played the part of Arnie's pretend wife.
At one point she tries to kill him.

At the end of filming
Sharon could buy the house she wanted
and that's what she did.

With Arnold Schwarzenegger in *Total Recall*.

Soon after *Total Recall*
she was in a bad car crash.
The doctor said
it was only the training for the film
that saved Sharon from being in a wheelchair.

After the crash,
Sharon spent time planning her career.
Total Recall was a success
but people didn't know her name.
She needed publicity.

At the age of 32 she posed for *Playboy* magazine.
They sold out.
That copy is now a collector's item.

For the next two years
Sharon didn't get the success she wanted.
She wasn't playing dumb blondes
but the scripts were still poor.

One day she got a call
from the director of *Total Recall*.

6   *Basic Instinct*

They were making a film called *Basic Instinct*.
Michael Douglas was the star.
They needed a leading lady
but many actresses
had turned the film down.
Sharon was not the first choice.
She was not Michael Douglas' choice.
Later they all said
that they were wrong.

Basic Instinct is a sexy thriller.
It's about a cop looking for a killer.
Sharon plays the main suspect.

The film was a risk for Sharon Stone.
She took the risk.
As she said,
'Time was running out
and I needed to be a film star'.
Basic Instinct did make her a star.
In the UK it was the top film of 1992.

In the film *Basic Instinct*.

7 The Critics

There was a down side
to Sharon's success.
She was followed everywhere.
The newspapers said she took drugs.

She said,
'In Hollywood, you can be
tall, blonde and pretty –
but you can't be smart.'

Quietly, Sharon and her sister Kelly
set up a hostel for abused children.
Every year they take the children
on holiday.
The newspapers don't talk about this.

Sharon's next film was called *Sliver*.
This time she was not the killer.
She was the victim.
The film was going to be a blockbuster.
It was a shock to everyone
when the critics didn't like it.

Added to this, Sharon had an affair
with the producer of *Sliver*.
The newspapers called her a home breaker.

Sliver made money at the box office
and this kept Sharon at the top.

The critics hated her next three films.
They rubbished them in the newspapers.
They didn't make money
and her career was in crisis.

Then she heard about a film called *Casino*
and Robert De Niro was the star.
This was Sharon's dream come true.

She wanted the part of Ginger,
a pill-popping, gold digger.
Ginger is De Niro's wife.
Sharon didn't mind what she was paid.
She said she would do the film
for next to nothing.
She got the part.

Sharon threw herself
into this part.
She had a lot of fun.
At the end of filming
Sharon was given all the clothes
that she wore.
They cost over $1 million.

Sharon with Robert De Niro in *Casino* – a dream come true!

The critics liked her work in *Casino*.
She won a Golden Globe Award
for best actress in 1997.
Sharon felt that she
had arrived as a top actress.

Sharon formed her own
production company.
She called it *Chaos*.
This didn't help with
her next two films.

The critics who liked her work in *Casino*
were quick to blame her
when she didn't have one success after another.

Having a flop did not stop Sharon
from being a Hollywood star.
She acted like the Hollywood stars of old.
She made clever use of publicity.

Clever publicity
did not save her next film in 1998.
It had a famous cast
but again, a bad script.
It was called *Sphere*.

It was about a group of scientists
going to the ocean floor
to look at a crashed space ship.
The critics said,
'Water load of rubbish, a great cast wasted.'

8 Wedding Bells

1998 did have a
personal high point for Sharon.
She got married on Valentine's Day.
She married Phil,
the editor of a San Francisco newspaper.

Sharon wore a beautiful
pink dress for her wedding.
They had a big party at her house
in Beverly Hills.

Sharon with Phil at the Cannes Film Festival, May 1998.

Sharon had three more tries
for success in 1999.
She made a thriller,
a comedy and a drama.

In the meantime
Sharon speaks her mind
and takes risks.
The risks don't always pay off
but when they do
her acting skills are there to see.

Sharon Stone

Julia Holt

ems:

Published in association with The Basic Skills Agency

Hodder & Stoughton

A MEMBER OF THE HODDER HEADLINE GROUP

Acknowledgements

Cover: All Action

Photos: pp 2, 15, 19, 23 Moviestore; p 5 Frank Spooner; p 9 Camerapress;
p 12 Allstar; p 27 Topham Picturepoint

Every effort has been made to trace copyright holders of material reproduced in this book. Any rights not acknowledged will be acknowledged in subsequent printings if notice is given to the publisher.

Orders; please contact Bookpoint Ltd, 39 Milton Park, Abingdon, Oxon OX14 4TD. Telephone: (44) 01235 400414, Fax: (44) 01235 400454. Lines are open from 9.00–6.00, Monday to Saturday, with a 24 hour message answering service.
Email address: orders@bookpoint.co.uk

British Library Cataloguing in Publication Data
A catalogue record for this title is available from the British Library

ISBN 0 340 77622 6

First published 2000
Impression number   10 9 8 7 6 5 4 3 2 1
Year   2005 2004 2003 2002 2001 2000

Typeset by GreenGate Publishing Services, Tonbridge, Kent.
Printed in Great Britain for Hodder and Stoughton Educational, a division of Hodder Headline Plc, 338 Euston Road, London NW1 3BH, by Redwood Books, Trowbridge, Wilts